This Literary Life

PETER VAN STRAATEN

COFFEE HOUSE PRESS :: MINNEAPOLIS :: 1991

Thanks go to The Bush Foundation, Northwest Area Foundation, and Elmer L. and Eleanor J. Andersen for supporting this project.

Coffee House Press books are available to bookstores through our primary distributor, Consortium Book Sales & Distribution, 287 East Sixth Street, Suite 365, St. Paul, Minnesota 55101. Our books are also available through all major library distributors and jobbers, and through most small press distributors, including Bookpeople, Bookslinger, Inland, Pacific Pipeline, and Small Press Distribution. For personal orders, catalogs, or other information, write to:

COFFEE HOUSE PRESS
27 North Fourth St., Suite 400, Minneapolis, MN 55401

Library of Congress Cataloging in Publication Data

Straaten, Peter van.
    This literary life / Peter van Straaten.
      p. cm.
    ISBN 0-918273-92-7 (PBK.): $7.50
     1. Litterateurs – Caricatures and cartoons. 2. Dutch wit and
    humor. Pictorial. I. Title.
    NC1549.S8A41991
    741.5'9492 – DC20

                         91-4969
                          CIP

This Literary Life

" WHY ISN'T MY BOOK NEXT TO THE CASH REGISTER? "

"I BET ANY OTHER PUBLISHER WOULD HAVE MADE THIS A BESTSELLER YEARS AGO"

"WHO WERE YOU THINKING OF WHEN YOU
WROTE THAT EROTIC PASSAGE?"

" NO, ADAM! JUST CORRECT THE PROOFS!
I FORBID YOU TO REWRITE THE WHOLE BOOK!"

"YOU KNOW WHAT IT IS ABOUT HER BOOKS?
I ALWAYS THINK, IF ONLY
I COULD WRITE LIKE HER......
I'D DO IT COMPLETELY DIFFERENTLY"

"SO WRITE FEWER POEMS THIS YEAR, JACK.
WHO CARES? "

"WELL? DID YOU LIKE IT? DID IT MAKE
YOU LAUGH IN PLACES?"

"NOT GOING SO WELL, EH?
AS FAR AS WE'RE CONCERNED
YOU CAN GO HOME AN HOUR EARLY"

"OF COURSE YOU CAN DO IT!
IT'LL BE TERRIFIC!
I CAN FEEL IT IN MY BONES!"

" AGAIN ?
WHAT ON EARTH DO YOU DO WITH
ALL THOSE ADVANCES ? "

"AH ... FINISHED YOUR CHAPTER?
FINISHED THE BOOK? OR ARE YOU STUCK?"

"I GIVE UP, PAUL. YOU'VE WRITTEN A
COMPLETELY DIFFERENT BOOK AGAIN
COULDN'T YOU REPEAT YOURSELF
ONCE IN A WHILE?"

"MAKE SURE YOU PUT IN A COUPLE OF
PASSAGES THAT THE READER CAN SKIP"

"IDIOT! YOU'RE BURSTING WITH TALENT!"

"OH NO, IT DOESN'T HURT A BIT. ON THE
CONTRARY. I'D HATE TO HAVE HIS SUCCESS"

"YOU KNOW A BOOK I THINK'S **FANTASTIC**?
WAR AND PEACE.
WHY DON'T YOU WRITE SOMETHING LIKE THAT?"

" YOU'RE A POET, TOM.
DON'T EVER FORGET IT "

" I'VE READ IT. I THINK IT'S MORE FOR GRAYWOLF "

"I HEAR THAT YOUR PIECES ARE GETTING
BETTER ALL THE TIME. WE'LL HAVE
TO DO AN ANTHOLOGY ONE OF THESE DAYS"

"JACK, WHY DON'T I CALL THE EDITOR AND SAY THAT FOR HEALTH REASONS YOU REFUSE TO REVIEW NORMAN MAILER?"

"I HAVE TO BE STRAIGHT WITH YOU, HANNAH.
YOU'RE SIMPLY NOT CAPABLE OF WRITING A POT-BOILER."

"AH....YOUR NEW BOOK! RIGHT ON TIME!
NICE AND SLEAZY AGAIN, I HOPE ?"

"THEY SAY YOU'RE THE NEW BILL MOYERS"

"PERHAPS YOU SHOULD TURN DOWN
ANOTHER PRIZE, BILL...."

"BIT OF A NERD, BUT HE'S ONE OF OUR MOST
PROMISING READERS."

"THE REVIEWER'S RIGHT, VICKY.....
I SHOULDN'T HAVE WRITTEN THAT BOOK"

"ISN'T IT GREAT? ONLY TWO
CHAPTERS TO GO!"

"THERE! I'VE WRITTEN ANN'S FORWORD AS SHE
ASKED....IT MAKES HER WHOLE BOOK SUPERFLUOUS!"

"GOD, IF ONLY S.J. PERELMAN WERE STILL ALIVE!"

"WELL? PRETTY WILD, DON'T YOU THINK?"

"NOW YOU'LL DEDICATE YOUR NEXT
BOOK TO ME, WON'T YOU?"

"SO TELL ME ... ARE YOU AN
IMPORTANT POET?"

"TONY, REMIND ME ...THAT POEM OF YOURS THAT WAS IN GRANTA THE OTHER WEEK, HOW DID IT GO AGAIN ?"

"IF EVERYTHING WORKS OUT, YOU COULD
BE OUR NEW HEMINGWAY!"

"GOOD GOD, YVONNE...THERE'S NO NEED
TO SUFFER WITH EVERY SINGLE POET."

"THREE HUNDRED COPIES IS A SUCCÈS
D'ESTIME, TONY, A SUCCÈS D'ESTIME"

"MOM! YOU CAN FORGET DAD FOR A WHILE....
HE'S GIVING BIRTH TO A NEW NOVEL!"

"ALL THAT HEGEL CRAP. WHO NEEDS IT ?"

"WELL, IT'S STILL NOT **QUITE** EIGHT O'CLOCK..."

"BUT **I** BELIEVE IN YOU, FRANK!"

"I THINK THIS TIME I'LL TRY WRITING
A REALLY FEMININE BOOK."

"AND I SUPPOSE IT'S ALSO MY FAULT YOU
DIDN'T WIN THE NOBEL?"

"OH DARLING ... YOU'VE ABSOLUTELY
PERFECTED THE ART OF LEAVING THINGS OUT!"

"DON'T TED. I ADMIRE YOU AS A WRITER.
BUT THAT'S IT."

"GOOD GRIEF, EMMA ... IS IT **THAT** BADLY WRITTEN?"

"BILL, I'VE DECIDED TO WRITE FOR A
SMALLER AUDIENCE FROM NOW ON."

"I'M LEAVING YOU, CHRISTOPHER.
I DON'T FIT YOUR LIST ANYMORE"

" I HAD TO LAUGH AT THAT FOOL'S BOOK.
WHY DON'T I PUT: " NOT UNAMUSING" ? "

"IF YOU'VE FINISHED WRITING YOUR TRILOGY, WOULD YOU PLEASE TAKE OUT THE TRASH?"

"LOVE AND SEX PLAY A MINOR ROLE IN
YOUR NEW BOOK. WHY IS THAT?"

"I STILL DON'T KNOW WHAT YOU THINK OF MY POEMS"

"I WOULDN'T LOSE ANY SLEEP OVER IT, IF
I WERE YOU...WHO IS THIS GORE VIDAL ANYWAY?"

"FINISH YOUR BOOK FIRST, JACK.....
THEN WE'LL DO LUNCH ....."

"ALL RIGHT, MAYBE HER POEMS ARE WORTHLESS,
BUT WE COULD USE A POLITICALLY CORRECT
FEMINIST FOR THE LIST "

"NORTH DAKOTA? THE BOOK'S SET IN NORTH DAKOTA? MY GOD. IT CAN'T BE UP TO MUCH."

"I'D GIVE UP, IF I WERE YOU. HARDLY
ANYTHING MAKES HAROLD BLOOM LAUGH."

"I'M WARNING YOU, JAMES! YOU'RE NOT TO START ANY FURTIVE POEM-WRITING HERE!"

"COME ON, DICK ....WHY NOT ADMIT THAT MARTY'S RIGHT.... FREUD ISN'T WORTH THE PAPER HE'S PRINTED ON."

"YOU MUST GET YOUR MAIN CHARACTER TO DO
    SOMETHING NOW AND THEN, STEVEN."

"SUCH A SHAME THIS IS YOUR FOURTH NOVEL! IT WOULD HAVE BEEN **THE** DEBUT OF 1992."

"HUH! .... MACHO!"

"I'M SORRY TO CALL SO LATE, RICHARD, BUT
WE WERE THINKING AT THE EDITORIAL
MEETING..... SHOULDN'T YOU BE CONTRIBUTING
SOMETHING ABOUT SARTRE TOO?"

"INSPIRATION? FOR WRITERS LIKE ME,
IT JUST GETS IN THE WAY."

" YOU KNOW WHAT BUGS ME MOST
ABOUT WRITING? IT'S JUST WORK! "

"HAVE A DRINK WITH ME, SWEETHEART....
I'M CELEBRATING TWENTYFIVE YEARS
OF BEING A PROMISING WRITER"